LITTLE BOOK OF
MEDITATIONS, VOLUME ONE

LITTLE BOOK OF MEDITATIONS, VOLUME ONE

YOUR KEY TO PEACE AND HAPPINESS IN TURBULENT TIMES

DEBBRA LUPIEN

LUPIEN LIMITED

Lupien Limited

Cresco, PA 18326

Cover Image by AdelinaZw from Pixabay

Spiritual Enlightenment Series

Little Book of Meditations, Volume One/ Debbra Lupien — 1st ed.

Library of Congress Control Number: TBA

ISBN 978-0-9994880-5-8 (Kindle)

ISBN 978-0-9994880-7-2 (Paperback)

CONTENTS

To Archangel Metatron, my mentor and BFF. Thank you for your love, support and guidance, every step of the way. Your steadfast presence in my life has made all the difference. You ARE the great transformer.

A NOTE FROM THE AUTHOR

The inspiration to share meditations in written form came about because I always find myself anticipating what's next during guided meditations.

Distracted thoughts lead to not relaxing for the full benefit.

Reading first means you'll know what's coming so that when you listen, voíla, you're relaxed and in the flow.

Yes, listen, because I've *recorded* all the meditations for you. (See the *Meditation Audios* page for more information.)

ABOUT THE MEDITATIONS

All meditations, *by energetic intention*, take place in the safety of your Akashic Records so that you can fully relax, knowing you're in the capable hands of your personal Akashic team.

You'll notice some begin with a grounding, as it was part of the vision, while others do not. When there's no grounding, please feel free to insert your own favorite, or use the grounding from Chapter One.

The order of meditations is purposeful, as specified by Metatron. However, you may use them in any order you choose. Let your intuition guide the way.

You'll find meditations for a variety of situations, so that there will always be a convenient meditation tool at your disposal.

While some put more focus on healing, like Chapter Six, there are healing elements to all, as being in the fifth dimension *is* healing and rejuvenating.

The more complex meditations lean towards teaching a lesson, rather than visualization journeys. That is very purposeful on Metatron's part, to facilitate your consciousness expansion. Others, like Chapter 17, are both spiritual lesson, and guided visualization.

After you've read, listened and have the rhythm of a meditation, allow yourself to expand upon the experience in subsequent listening. The original is your springboard to even more expansive soul journeys.

One day, you may discover that you no longer need the audio, because your meditation muscle is toned and ready to go.

After you've read, listened and have the rhythm of a meditation, allow yourself to expand upon the experience in subsequent listening. The original is your springboard to even more expansive soul journeys.

Understand that when you go through your Akashic Records to have these fifth-dimensional experiences, they *are* real. As real as your third-dimensional life.

In the fifth dimension, everything happens at the speed of thought. Becoming accustomed to that way of being will translate to a more soul satisfying life here on Earth.

As your consciousness expands, so too does your third-dimensional self. Stepping into the consciousness of an unlimited, sovereign soul is the next evolution of humanity.

You, Dear Beautiful Soul, are at the forefront of that transformation. Thank you for being a part of the *great shift* that will bring forth Earthtopia.

At the time of this writing (late 2022), the planet was moving towards the end of a global pandemic, which accounts for certain references you'll find throughout.

ONE FINAL NOTE

The *Introduction, Epilogue,* and *Afterword* are each channeled messages from Metatron, specifically for this book and you.

While reading, you may find yourself caught up in the meditations and miss these important messages. That would be a shame.

MEDITATION AUDIOS

The meditations were individually recorded and are available at
debbralupien.com/voice. You may listen to them in order, or select
them as you feel inspired.

To enhance your experience, I highly recommend you read the
meditation before listening.

INTRODUCTION

In this time of great upheaval and chaos, we, your angels, want you to know we are always by your side. There is nothing you have done, or could ever do to change that truth.

You are worthy of our ministrations, and we are committed to you.

We recognize that sometimes you feel bereft, as if you were adrift at sea. That separateness is an illusion. During those times, it is incumbent upon you to call out for assistance so that we may serve.

No need is too great or too small. We may not deliver exactly what you request, but we will always deliver exactly what you need in the moment.

Therefore, it would be wise to push away fear and doubt. Do not waste even a moment of your time engaged in those negative energies, which cause you to feel separated.

Instead, lean into the loving arms of your angel team. Allow them to soothe and comfort so that you might stand tall and strong, no matter what challenge comes your way.

Yes, there will be huge challenges ahead, but you are ready to meet them as you stand steadfast in the knowledge that you *are* a sovereign soul, and a powerful lightworker come to usher in the enlightened age of Earthtopia.

We promise, all of your efforts will be worth it. Meanwhile, there is much work to be done. See to your own needs with diligence as you expand your consciousness and raise your vibrational frequency.

That is not to say your days must be all work. No, far from it. While you are on the path to Earthtopia, you must also be mindful of your personal soul journey. Lean into what feeds your soul and don't forget to weave in strands of fun.

Earthtopia is the big, collective picture. However, it should not eclipse your personal journey. Both are equally important.

Have faith and trust that as a beloved child of Creator you have what it takes to see this challenge through to completion, and you can have a splendid life while doing it. The two are not mutually exclusive.

Revel in the abundant opportunities available to you as an unbounded, limitless soul.

We know you do not always feel that, nevertheless; it is true. Consider how you might allow it to feel true.

Should you need more angel help, then ask for more. Angel assistance is limitless.

Would you like an entire squadron? Then ask. Yes, it is entirely within your authority as a sovereign soul to invoke a squadron!

What kind of angels would you like? Warriors, help mates, performers? Think about that, then call upon exactly the type of angel you need. Remember, this is your reality, so make it a good one.

You will find in the pages of this book fanciful, meditative journeys. It is our intent to inspire you into more expansive dreams. The time to play small has long passed.

Spread your wings and fly like a beautiful butterfly, or a powerful hawk. Yes, you really can do that on your meditative journeys, where change happens at the speed of thought.

As you process each experience, we encourage you to write down new insights, ahas, or inspired thoughts. Words, thoughts, or feelings that may not make sense today may one day connect with others to deliver a massive wisdom nugget.

Now, we invite you to explore these pages. Allow yourself to relax into each journey, expand your consciousness and understanding about the sparkling, soul satisfying possibilities that await you. Then, go out there and create something phenomenal.

With deep, abiding love and admiration,

Archangel Metatron and the gang

GROUNDING

*T*his is a basic grounding exercise that you can use before any meditation. Grounding is an important step to ensure you stay connected to present reality, whilst energetically traveling in other dimensions.

———◦⟨∞⟩◦———

When you're ready, sit back, close your eyes, and take a couple of deep breaths. Relax and focus on your breathing as you slip into a deeply relaxed state.

Let all thoughts and worries that came with you today slide away. Mother Earth will absorb them, leaving you light and free.

Now with your eyes still closed, look up and notice a pillar of white, brilliant light descending towards you. Coming closer and closer until it reaches your crown chakra, where it enters your body, very gently sliding down over your face, past your neck, resting lightly on your shoulders.

Notice it expanding to encompass your entire body as it slides down your abdomen, your hips, legs, all the way down until it reaches the ground.

You are now ensconced in this beautiful white pillar of light.

You may feel a little tingle in your body as you light up with the love and healing energy of Divine. Know that you are safe in this place.

It's a beautiful feeling as the light ignites your senses and neural pathways. Absorb all of that love and know that you are a child of the Divine. You are perfect. You are magnificent.

There's nothing wrong with you. You're not broken. You never were.

When you tune in and take advantage of the love and power that's being shared with you minute by minute, second by second, from your Creator, you have everything you need.

Now, take a second to thank Divine, and your angels, for all that they have done and all that they *will* do.

When you're ready, open your eyes and come fully back to present awareness.

LOVE IS THE ANSWER TO EVERYTHING

This powerful grounding begins with a double lightning bolt that feels as if it's piercing your skull then runs quickly through your entire body.

As the energy nears the bottom of your feet, it slows, transforms to liquid, and flows gently into the ground.

When the last bit of liquid disappears, a vine erupts from the ground and slowly winds its way up, through your body, out of your crown chakra, into the heavens, leaving you safely suspended between Creator and Earth.

At first, you experience a feeling of being trapped and reflexively struggle. Your angels quickly reassure you that all is as it should be, allowing you to relax, knowing that despite appearances, you're safe, protected and loved.

No need to struggle or be afraid. This is your support system which assists you through challenging times, until you're strong enough to support yourself. Your smallest needs are met, just as they always have been, and always shall be.

Feeling your way through the present situation, you discover that you're weightless, and have the ability to fly, even with your vine attachment.

The vine flows with you. A reminder of this Universal truth: Creator is on the job, today, yesterday and all of your tomorrows. Nary a moment goes by that you are not safe and secure within the bosom of Divine... loved, cherished, safe.

You may sever the ties a million times, yet they remain, for Divine will *never* desert you. Like the prodigal, you are always welcomed back with open arms.

Creator's love is steadfast and permanent. It will never fade, nor will it end. Nothing you do will ever change that timeless truth.

Know this: **Love is the answer to everything.**

Love of self, complete and total acceptance of the marvel that you are. Once embodied, turn your love and acceptance outward. Share this Divine truth with whomever will listen. One person sharing with another until love is tangible, pervasive and *felt*!

Love is the key to creating your maximum impact; to self and to others, cascading across your world like dominoes. A perfectly arranged cascade of dominoes, sending massive ripples across the land; calling more souls to awaken, more souls to feel the love and pass it on.

This is the *Cosmic Wave of Transformation*. For, when love replaces hate, fear, and mistrust, people everywhere will align with this singular purpose. Then watch as the waves of love transform one person after another.

Come child, board the love train.

Be a part of something greater than yourself, exquisitely rewarding. This is the way to transform your world into a collective cooperative where love flows like water.

Allow our love message to reverberate through your entire being, filling you to overflowing.

Notice how the energy flows over, around, and through your body, igniting your senses, and your passion. You're filled with a desire to be more, and do more on this amazing, consequential soul journey.

Stay in this delightful energy for as long as you like.

When you are ready, the vine will recede. Watch as it slowly unwinds down your body until it reaches the ground and disappears from sight.

Slowly bring your awareness back to the present to process this experience.

SACRED TIME WITH THE DIVINE

*T*his grounding begins with a powerful force that almost slams into your head — then abruptly stops. The feeling is that of one immovable force meeting another — your resistance.

Then, as all resistance slowly melts away, you find yourself encased in a beautiful light, your body levitates in the center. It's beautiful, gentle and peaceful. Incredibly relaxing.

There you are floating without a care in the world. Secure in the understanding that you are ensconced in the arms of the angels, safe, loved and cherished.

You're so relaxed that it would take tremendous effort to lift your arm. But you don't want to. You only want to stay in this peaceful zone of love and protection as you invite Divine to commune with you.

This is your sacred time with Divine.

Soak up the healing, re-energizing light until you're filled to over-flowing. Abundance is the hallmark of the Divine. Pouring love and light upon you in a never-ending stream.

It's only incumbent upon you to open up and receive. The flow will never end. It is you who becomes embroiled in cares and woes who turn away. But the magnificent, amazing truth is that the light is always there waiting to pick up where you left off.

If life has taken you far from your intended spiritual pursuits, do not excoriate yourself. That only serves to move you further away. Instead, turn your eyes back to the light, and with a big smile upon your face, run towards it.

Allow it to penetrate every fiber of your being. To restore your vitality, your hope, your divine inner light. Soak it in for as long as you like, knowing you can return to this space in a moment. It is always here for you.

Better yet, make it a regular practice to come back to this space and recharge. Do not wait until you are depleted. You will find this practice incredibly helpful in maintaining your positive outlook and peaceful countenance.

From this space of Zen, you will have greater insight. All the fuzziness and static of your bustling reality will fade away, allowing more clarity than you thought possible.

It is an immutable fact that if you do not fill the gas tank on your motor vehicle, it will simply cease functioning.

Fortunately for you, the energy that animates your third-dimensional body will sustain you in a limited capacity, even if you neglect to refill. However, that is putting undue stress upon yourself, and so unnecessary.

Divine will never give up on you. It is you who sometimes gives up on yourself. No matter how bleak the outlook, you can turn things around by focusing upon your purpose and showing up at the Divine filling station to top off your tank.

How wonderful that you don't have to drive miles and miles on empty to locate the nearest station. No, all you need do is stop and allow it to come to you. How marvelous is that? Can you feel the love that surrounds you even now?

It never leaves you. It is you that leaves. When you finally understand this truth and allow the Divine filling station to come to you, your life will never be the same in the most marvelous way.

Imagine each day waking up, topping off your energetic tank, then excitedly going out into the world to discover what new delights await.

Even those tasks that are not the most joyful will be easier when you perform them from this state of peace, bliss and understanding. Your heart will beat with love and gratitude for all that you have and all that you are.

Imagine how being in this state will impact those around you. They can't help but be positively impacted. Little by little, they will shift, and soon they will impact those around them. As you share your new understanding of *being* more, even more souls will awaken to this truth, creating a massive ripple across your world. How delicious is that?

Can you imagine that sort of world? Do you even now scoff that it's impossible?

We understand. That is a mighty big vision, but we assure it is possible, and it has happened in other places at other times. We have witnessed many awakenings, both great and small. They are a marvel to behold and we celebrate each one.

It is a joyous occasion when souls experience a rapid growth spurt on their journey to higher consciousness.

We see so many of you who have been valiantly trying to surf the wave of cosmic transformation. Sometimes you manage to make your way atop the wave for brief moments. Remember how that felt?

Focus on reveling in your accomplishment rather than upon your disappointment when you fall. That's how you learn. We will never give up on you. Please don't give up on yourself.

You are so close to a breakthrough.

Just like a child learning to walk, keep getting back up and try again. Focus on how good it feels each time you stand. Allow that feeling to help keep you moving forward.

Each time you rise up, there is an energetic shift. You *are* moving closer to that which you seek. When you need help ask, we are always here.

<hr>

Now, Dear One, your sacred time with Divine draws to a close. Take a couple of deep breaths and bring your awareness back to the present.

MINI MEDITATIVE MOMENTS

*I*magine a blanket of Divine love and light wrapping you in a cocoon. There you feel warm and filled with goodness, laughter, and a sense of adventure. A sense of knowing something great is coming. A feeling of anticipation shivers up your back because the energies have been building and building for quite some time.

You are living in a time when a crescendo point draws near. Life is going to be more interesting — opportunities abound like sand on the beach. During this time, it's incumbent upon you to relax, and be open to the experience. The way to do that is to be present in the moment.

Avoid the frenetic rush and worry that occupies a great many of Earth's citizens. Because, if you're so minutely involved in everyday life, worried about deadlines and appointments, it's like wearing blinders, making you unaware of the bread crumbs your angels are constantly presenting to help and inspire you.

Make it your practice to pause and take a few deep breaths several times throughout the day. A teeny, tiny, mini meditation.

In that breathing moment, look around and take note of what you see. If you notice a pattern showing up, that's a clue to stop and take a slightly longer meditative break.

Allow an inspired idea to come into your awareness; because it's right there on the edge of your consciousness, waiting to break through.

Give it a moment to come through.

The more often you do this, the easier it will get to receive angelic messages.

Create a new discipline of periodically pausing. Slow down and notice the messages that have been there all along waiting for you to receive.

Your angels jump up and down for joy, celebrating your break-through.

Now, they'll scatter even more breadcrumbs for your consideration. And so it goes, until one day you're seeing breadcrumbs and receiving messages with ease; because you're more present all of the time.

That's the reality you're working towards. Don't worry about being perfect, obviously you're human, not perfect.

Make this your new routine:

As you go about your day, stop once in a while. Pause and be present. Pay attention to what's going on in your world.

Watch for Divine inspiration. When you see/hear/feel it, make a note. Put it in your phone, or record it in some fashion, whatever you have to do so you don't forget. Inspired insights are fleeting, almost like butterfly kisses. You'll feel them momentarily then they're gone.

Should you continue to miss them, they'll get a little stronger. But, wouldn't it be wonderful if you got them in the moment of the *butterfly kiss*, because then you'll get more.

The sooner you receive and take action, the sooner you'll get more. Your life will rapidly move in a more positive direction. You'll see more of what you desire coming to fruition.

And now, let's take this experience full circle. Bring your awareness back to the blanket of Divine love and light cocooning your body. Revel in the safe, secure feeling of being a cherished, beloved child of the Divine.

PREPARE YE THE WAY — PANDEMIC MEDITATION

*T*uning into the energy of the global pandemic, there's a denseness, like trying to run through water. You feel pressure on your chest and your breathing is restricted.

You wonder: Is this an empathic reaction to those who struggle with virus symptoms?

Is this part of ascension? If so, what is the best course of action?

Have no fear. It's important to gain a greater understanding of this planetary shared experience.

Sitting quietly, reflecting upon these questions brings a lightening of the intense pressure, along with the knowing that self care is part of the larger message.

As you continue contemplating, allow Divine to lift all your burdens and worry.

Focus in faith and trust that there is indeed a higher power at work on your behalf.

Sit quietly. Breathe, relax, allow.

Listen and feel for what message comes. Then record it — even if it seems like random thoughts from your own brain.

These thoughts act as your way shower. Follow them and see where they lead. They're priming the pump, providing structure and direction, paving the way for the Divine stream of consciousness that is coming.

As you process these thoughts, you hear the song: *Prepare Ye The Way* from Godspell. (1971 Stephen Schwarz musical)

Yes, *you're* preparing the way to be more in alignment, more at peace, more deeply connected to the Source of all that is.

That is the perpetual desire of your soul, but that is an illusion, for *you were never disconnected.*

Creator has always been at your side. It is *you* who puts up walls, disconnects, or gets lost in a sea of swirling cares and woes.

That is also an illusion, one of your own making. Therefore, you have the power to release it, to be replaced by love and light, that joyous connection to the Source of all.

As you process these truths, your chest feels lighter, breathing is now easier, calmness and peace wash over you as your thoughts return to knowing that all really is right with the world — despite outward appearances.

There *is* a plan at work. Do not allow yourself to be pulled under by the strong current of unenlightened thoughts and beliefs. Rise above. Tread water and float until you reach the other side.

Faith and perseverance will see you through, whether in your third-dimensional form, or upon a return to fifth-dimensional form. If that is your soul's intent at this time, it is perfect.

The souls who choose to remain behind during this pandemic, do so of their own free will. They knew it would not be easy, but they also knew that it would be an opportunity for spiritual growth.

Those who exited also did so of their own free will. They'll be back to carry on when the time is right for them. It's all perfect from the soul's perspective.

You need not exert energy worrying about them. This is their choice, and so shall it be.

If your choice is to remain behind, then it would best serve you to get on with your journey. There are great challenges yet to be navigated. Fear not, you are up to the challenge or you wouldn't be here seeking answers.

Know that your angels are ever on call to lead you through a crisis, just as they have ever done.

Lean on them. Call out to them. Ask for more help if it's needed. More will come at your call. There is a limitless supply of angels waiting to assist.

Except, they can't help if you don't ask. Call, and call frequently. Even if it's just to express your gratitude.

The more you connect with your angels, the easier it will become to connect with them. Allow them to fulfill their purpose by serving you.

Selah, Amen and Amen.

HEALING LOVE INFUSION —
HEART CHAKRA EXPANSION

*S*it back, close your eyes, wiggle your fingers and your toes as you settle in and get comfy in your space.

Begin by taking some deep, cleansing breaths, releasing all thoughts and cares of the day. (Pause)

Now, as you continue breathing normally, focus on the life-giving breath flowing through your entire body as any tightness or tension seeps out of your body and flows down into mother earth nurturing and leaving you deeply relaxed.

With your eyes still closed, look up and notice a flaming ball, high in the sky above. This ball is intense, bright and moving slowly down towards you.

It fascinates. You can't take your eyes off of this object, which looks like a multitude of threads woven together into a magnificent, flaming, orange/yellow/red ball.

The ball looks like it might be hot to the touch, and as it moves still closer, you feel the warmth. A warm, gentle, loving feeling emanates from the ball. Revel in the deliciousness of the moment.

Now the light and warmth are beaming onto your entire body, and as that big, flaming ball reaches the top of your head, making contact, there's a little jolt of electricity.

You might feel some tingling in your limbs as the ball moves down through your brain, lighting up the neurons. Then continuing down through your throat, chest, and slowly past your abdomen and hips.

The ball continues moving down your legs, and then finally all the way down to the bottoms of your feet, where it exits into the ground, gently slipping into the earth.

In your mind's eye, you see the ball moving further through the ground while the woven strands begin to unwind. The strands reach down to connect with the roots of trees, intertwining, and securing. You're now safely tethered betwixt Earth and Divine by these flaming threads. You'e safe and stable. You can completely relax and trust in this Divine space.

Pause for a moment to experience whatever sensations or feelings are present.

Know that whatever you experience, it is perfect.

Your attention is drawn to your heart chakra where you feel a tingly, bubbly sensation. Like little carbonation bubbles, lighting you up.

Dear Beautiful Soul, in this moment your heart chakra is expanding as it prepares to send love and healing to the entire world, but most importantly, love and healing to you!

The sensation is like being wrapped in the warmest, coziest, blanket of Divine love. Feel the warmth, rejuvenating, tingling through your body as you find yourself cocooned in a beautiful, cushiony blanket of Divine love.

You are being transformed. Your body is being infused with ener-gizing, Divine love, and light. As it flows through your body, it is seeking out any areas of disease or pain, replacing them with love and light. Sparkling, tingling, love and light.

Just allow that feeling to expand throughout your entire body.

As you relax in your cocoon, feeling safe, loved, and warm, you notice a movement off to your right.

A figure is approaching. You can't quite make out the shape, but it's white, and glows. As this figure comes closer, you now realize it is your Creator.

Your Creator, coming this day to make direct contact, reaching out beautiful arms to embrace you.

The feeling of being held in the arms of Creator is nearly indescribable. Elation, excitement, perhaps a little fear, and that's okay.

Just allow whatever you're feeling to flow and know that your Creator is really here.

You're receiving a special infusion of healing love, but more than that, you've received this magnificent, glowing ball of energy, absorbed into your body to be used as you move forward on your soul journey in any way you desire.

Because understand, Beautiful Soul, your journey is about doing what feeds your soul — always.

What lifts you up? What brings you bliss? That is your soul purpose.

When you do what feeds your soul, you'll bless and bring your light to the world. All light workers are being called. Come forth! You're needed.

This is your time.

Allow this infusion of Divine love and light to fill you with courage. To fill you with faith and trust. To fill you with the certainty that you *are* on your path. You *are* serving the higher good, and you *are* serving your own soul journey.

Still, the arms of Divine embrace you, feeling heavenly, warm, delicious, like drinking champagne when the bubbles tickle your nose. Delightful, and effervescent.

This is the energy Divine wants to imbue you with so you'll feel uplifted and buoyant.

Don't allow darkness to pull you down. Float above it. Know that if you feel it start to pull you down, all you need do is lift up your arms and call upon your angels.

They'll be right there, lifting you above the darkness, bringing you safely back to Earth in a new space, where you can continue sharing love and light which flows abundantly from you.

When you are filled with divine love, it spills over. It cannot be contained by your third-dimensional body. It *must* flow over and bless others, drawing them to you, so that you might share the amazing love light with them.

Now, Creator reaches out and gently touches your third eye. There's a jolt of powerful energy, like electricity, surging through your body. You might feel your limbs jerking, just a little, as your body accepts the flow of Divine energy.

Know that this is an infusion of even more power from Divine. It's coming in waves of ever higher frequency energy, to help you move forward on your new higher-purpose path.

All are being called to come together and lift up not only humanity, but earth herself.

So much excitement and bliss await you, Dear Beautiful Soul.

Do not fear. Step forward in confidence, knowing that you *are* firmly wrapped in the arms of your Creator. You *are* safe and secure; you *are* loved.

Just allow all of those feelings to surge through your body and process. However you're feeling is perfect. Know that when you complete this meditative journey, you'll retain uplifted energy which you may choose to share.

From this new place of empowerment, maintain a space of peace and serenity, because *this* is the *peace that passes understanding.*

The path to bliss and to living your purpose more fully than you ever have before.

Can you feel energy from your heart chakra expanding like the flaming ball? It grows brighter and brighter, so that those around you can't help but notice and be positively impacted. And the wonderful, magical part? You don't have to do *anything!*

Love and light will continue flowing from you unabated in waves, because you've been infused by Divine.

Also know, Dear Beautiful Soul, should you feel the need, you can come back to this space anytime for an overflow refill.

As the message completes, Creator bends down to kiss you on the forehead, blessing you to the highest, and assigning a trio of angels to stand with you on your sacred journey. (This is in addition to all the angels you already have.)

They will ever be at your side, and you can call for *more* anytime you wish. They're perpetually available in unlimited supply. *Do not hesitate to call.*

With that, Creator departs while the cocoon you've been wrapped in slowly opens.

You step out, feeling energized, and profoundly loved.

Words cannot adequately describe this amazing, uplifting feeling. You just want to sing. You're wearing an impossibly large smile, because everything feels so wonderful!

Now that you've stepped out of your cocoon, stretch your arms and legs, and slowly come back to present reality.

As you do, take note of the sensations coursing through your body. Remember this magnificent experience.

Now, take a couple of deep breaths, and when you're ready, open your eyes.

Welcome back, Beautiful. Don't forget to record the pertinent details of this experience. Then, you might want to spend a few minutes basking in gratitude to put the finishing touches on this journey.

RESETTING YOUR PHYSICALITY

a pillar of white light (looking like a portal) appears overhead and then very precisely beams down into your crown chakra. It feels cool, and somewhat surgical, as it moves through your body.

The light is bright, as if you were in the dark and someone suddenly turned on a searchlight, except the light is coming from within your body. You're lit from the inside out!

As you process this thought, understanding seeps in.

The pillar of light is a healing beam that, with laser-like precision, is excising unhealthy tissue, clearing away toxic materials as it irrigates your entire body.

This Divine beam is clearing away all the clutter and detritus. Not even the little stuck-on bits are a match for Divine cleansing.

You might say it's a *reset of your physicality.*

The beam, slowly and precisely, passes through every inch of your body.

Finally, having pushed all the darkness out ahead of it, the light exits through the soles of your feet in a sooty-looking poofy cloud that rapidly dissipates — the image is somewhat like a chimney sweep.

Having completed its work, the beam disappears.

Replacing the beam is a scene of you as a small child, visiting the doctor. The Dr. takes your temperature, gives you the once over and pronounces: *you're fine and should go play.*

So that's your Divine prescription:

Breathe, relax, allow, and receive the healing intended for you. Then, put all thoughts of fear and worry away to focus upon uplifting, playful thoughts. Shift your consciousness and energy towards light and well being.

That's the wise choice in this moment — and in every moment — really. For what you focus upon expands and persists. Let what persists be glowing, optimal health, peace and happiness.

And now, Beautiful Soul, your infant self has appeared, tenderly cradled in the arms of Creator, who is beaming down at your resplendence, pleased with who and what you are.

For, you are a much-beloved child of the Divine, today and every day. Nothing can, or will, ever change that truth.

Know it, feel it, believe it, for it is profound, sacred, and true.

As you gaze up into the eyes of Creator, you marvel at seeing your life reflected there.

You notice the times when Divine reached out to steady and encourage, or erupt in jovial belly laughs, at your antics.

You're touched to the core of your being as you realize that Creator is filled with love and gratitude for the magnificent masterpiece *YOU* are creating out of the raw materials you were given.

It has ever been thus. When you embody this truth and realize what a powerful creator *you* are, there will be no need to fret and worry. Your normal state of being will transform into peace and calm.

More of this, less of that — where *that* is fret and worry.

Breathe, relax, allow. Make it a song you sing every day, like the little bird chirping about the joy of life and love.

Soon, you'll notice others joining you, until there's a veritable flock of voices telegraphing their message of peace and love to the whole world.

In this way, you become a part of the movement to spread a *positive* infection across the world, replacing darkness, fear, and worry with peace, love, and light. This is the way you'll transform yourself and your world.

Selah/Amen

BLISS IN THE MIDST OF CHAOS

*T*his is a glorious day on Earth. We know for some people it might not seem like a glorious day, because there's so much swirling chaos, fear, and doubt. However, your angels want you to know *it's only temporary.*

Dear Beautiful Soul, you are experiencing today, in this very moment, the next evolutionary phase of humanity.

Evolution generally is not easy. It comes with some pain, as we've all observed, but know that it's for a greater purpose. Know beautiful child there's a pool of seething hate and bigotry writhing under your feet, disrupting your foundation, and infecting the weak. That darkness needs to be rooted out before you can realize the prophecy of Earthtopia.

Your Ascension, the next version of humanity, will be a golden age. Bigotry and hatred having been rooted out and transmuted to love, your world will be a veritable paradise.

You are presently moving into a phase of more joy, bliss, and cooperation with your fellow souls. In this new phase you'll be oblivious to skin color. You'll barely notice the physical form, because you will have transformed.

With your new, awakened vision, you'll see the resplendent soul that exists inside of the skin suits. We promise, when you look upon each other, soul to soul, you *will* be profoundly changed.

You can expect more love and cooperation for one another. Cooperation, collaboration, and exhilaration will become the norm. More opportunity, more insight, more wisdom, more more more!

Especially: more positive, uplifting golden Creator love light.

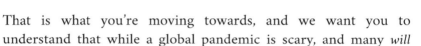

That is what you're moving towards, and we want you to understand that while a global pandemic is scary, and many *will* pass from this plane, it is all in Divine, perfect timing.

Understand that souls only depart the body when they're ready. The virus is simply a convenient means for a large number of souls to exit at this time. Those souls do not wish to remain behind to experience the growing pains of evolution.

That is perfect, because it's their soul's choice. They'll come back around again when they're ready.

To the beautiful light workers who choose to stay behind and do the heavy lifting, we send unceasing love and light. Know that we are here, supporting you, and lifting you up so that it need not be a struggle.

Know that while it might feel uncomfortable, remember our support. Allow us to help you through with more ease. When you do that, transformation will happen faster, and you'll arrive at the golden age sooner.

Trust us when we say, Earthtopia will be glorious!

As much as what you're experiencing now seems unthinkable, something you never dreamed you could experience in a dark way, what is coming for you on the other side is the polar opposite.

So amazing. So wonderful. So filled with love, delight, excitement, and exhilaration.

You will marvel at the extraordinary feeling and depth of beingness. Something you never imagined could be. Which, truly it couldn't have been in your old way of being.

So, as you ride the tsunami of this Cosmic Wave of Transformation, know that we've got you. We're supporting you. We're lifting you up.

Rock that wave, child! Enjoy it.

Yes, there is work. Yes, there is some struggle. But, change your perception and go with the flow, rather than fear what you have not yet experienced. Then it will be easier, better, and so much more comfortable.

Your transformation can be easy, like a dream, if you let it. Just flow with it. When you reach those moments where fear overtakes you, and feel you cannot stand it another minute, that's the time to *step back into your meditation.*

Let us lift you up and out of that space of fear. *Do not dance with darkness.* Do not stay in that place of fear.

As soon as you notice fear creeping in, take immediate action to step out of it, be diligent. We promise, the more you do that, the less often you'll find yourself in that dark space. One day fear will be totally washed away. You'll feel like you're floating on clouds. Life will be so easy and wonderful. *That's* what awaits you.

So, in this moment we call upon you to rise up in faith, strength, confidence, and understanding, that more and better is coming to you. Keep moving forward.

When you encounter an obstacle, do not despair. Simply move past the obstacle; whether that's over, around, or whether you call upon your angels to lift you up and carry you across. All things are possible.

Nothing can stop you, because you're on a Divinely guided soul journey. You *will* prevail. Just keep moving forward. As you do, reach out to those around you. Lift *them* up. If they haven't yet discovered this truth, share it with them. Share the love light. Bring them together as comrades in arms.

Walk together into your beautiful, bright future, filled with stunning, golden sunshine. That will light you up and clear away the darkness. Know that this is a time where collaboration, partnership, and teamwork is going to be more important than ever.

Yes, there will be some heavy lifting as you move into this new place. You're rebuilding from the very foundation. This time, that seething underbelly of hate and bigotry will not be there to corrupt your foundation. You'll be standing on the firm, beautiful, Divinely-guided foundation that will support you far into the future…

Until the day when you're ready for the next stage of human evolution — which will come all in good time.

Know that as you move away from this third-dimensional understanding of your world, it may take a while to get your sea legs, before you feel strong and confident. That's ok. Remember, babies have to crawl before they walk and run. But, run you will.

You're presently in the midst of a long marathon towards the next evolution of humanity, but you're ready. You've prepared for this. You would not have chosen to be here at this time if you were not strong enough and able to help usher in the new golden age.

Your angels are reaching out to you, encouraging you to hold their hands and let them lift you up in joy and light. Feel that love light penetrate your body. Feel it sinking deeply into your heart chakra, lighting you up from the inside out, filling you with an even higher quotient of Divine love and energy.

Feel it bursting from you in abundance as it spills over and touches those around you, inspiring and encouraging them. Together, Beautiful Souls, join hands and walk forward into your new awareness and the next level of evolution: Earthtopia.

With that, your angels gently kiss you on the third-eye, blessing you deeply, warming you all over. They bid you farewell, but just for this moment. Know that they are right there. Just call them and they'll be there.

Your angels say: please call us more. We have lots of time. In fact, we have an infinite amount of time for you, Dear Beautiful Child, because it's all about you and your journey.

We love you so very much. Come to the well often. Allow us to fill you up. That is our pleasure and privilege. In fact, it is our very purpose. Thank you for allowing us to help you.

And with that, the angels say amen and amen.

In case it's not obvious, the overriding message is reassurance that you can and will survive. You can do it the easy way or the hard way. Sinking into fear and chaos is the hard way.

Faith, trust, and leaning on your angels is the easy way.

The path you take is your choice. Choose wisely.

REST, REJUVENATION, ALLOWING

*I*t's raining gold glitter. Falling in straight lines that look like glitter curtains.

You face a dilemma.

You want to enter the inner sanctum, but don't want to get doused in glitter and there's no space to go around. What to do?

You *can* choose to wait and see if something changes, so that is what you decide to do.

Your choice made, a voice quietly says: "Don't rush into decisions. Consider carefully your options and then make the choice that best serves your *long-term* well being."

As those words seep into your consciousness, you experience a feeling that a big burden was just lifted.

Your body is totally relaxed, while the light grows dim.

Sleep, is calling your name. (Have you been getting enough sleep?)

Suddenly, you notice being so relaxed that you can barely lift your arms.

You feel yourself falling deeply into a pool of rest, relaxation, and rejuvenation.

As you lie back and absorb these sensations, sun breaks through the darkness. It's beaming down directly upon you.

Feel the warm, life-giving sun upon your face. The vitality spreads through your entire body, energizing and filling you with *vital force energy*.

This energy is so potent you feel as if you could bounce around like a puppet on a string.

You simply cannot remain still. (Feeling like hyperactivity.)

As the beam of energy subsides, calmness is restored. You're once more still, waiting. (Persist through the hyperactivity, calm *will* be restored.)

A voice shares this message: allow the life-giving energy to come to you. When it does, allow it to nourish your entire being. Absorb it and be renewed by it.

Allow it to sustain you as mother's milk once did.

Do not struggle — wait quietly and allow.

There is peace in the stillness if you will but allow.

Quiet your mind, focus on your breathing, and feel the sun's energy filling the empty tank of your being. It will fill you to the top if you let it.

Ask for vital force energy to come and fill you. Let it know that it's welcome and it will return as often as you desire. The power is yours, it always was.

Namasté

Notice the drum beat of allow flowing throughout this message? Allowing is an incredibly powerful spiritual principle. Divine, angels, and the spiritually minded can send you all manner of good things, but you must choose to receive else all of that marvelous energy will be blocked. Allow...

SACRED COMMUNION WITH
YOUR ANGELS

*S*tress, worry, fear. A feeling like an over-inflated balloon that suddenly pops under pressure.

The unexpected result is a feeling of extreme lightness. *Letting go of that which does not serve is the wisest choice.*

Do not concern yourself with that which is out of your control. Rest assured that your team is ever at the ready to shield, protect, and guide you every step of the way.

You are **NEVER** alone.

You are much loved, cherished, and respected for your braveness in undertaking the challenge of this third-dimensional plane.

Third-dimensional energy is highly dense in contrast to the fifth dimension from whence you came. That is why it's so vital that you securely ground yourself before connecting, lest you float right out of your body.

With this reminder, an incredible feeling of peacefulness floods over and through your being. Washing away distracting trials and tribulations, leaving you floating in the energy of pure bliss. This is the best method to right whatever is wrong or askew in your reality. This is the *peace that passeth understanding*.

Yes, third-dimensional issues still remain, however, they have shrunk in importance, and from this perspective will be easily resolved.

Revel in this exquisite experience, like floating in soothing, gentle water, a healing pool that cradles you, no need to even tread water. Allow the healing properties of this place to nourish and nurture you, body and soul.

This water is restorative and you may remain here for as long as you like. It is our gift to you. A sacred place to commune with your angels. For, in this place, you are fully attuned to our voices.

Relax, allow, breathe (Isn't that backwards? You wonder as a chuckle drifts past.)

Exactly! It's a mirror reflection. (Quiet laughter.)

Ah, now you understand. This space is a portal where the veil is whisper thin. That is why you may connect and hear your angels so perfectly here.

No struggle, not even to tread water. Just relax, allow, breathe, again and again, for as long as you wish.

Getting sleepy? No worries. Sleep if that is what you need. Remember, these waters are restorative. Slumber peacefully and allow us to caress your furrowed brow, imbuing you with Divine Creator love light.

As the gentle ripples rock your body, hearken back to a time when you were but a babe, being rocked by a loving parent or guardian. If not in this lifetime, then in another.

Allow yourself to reconnect with a memory. Soak it in. Add it to your treasure chest of cherished memories. Let it sustain you during times of trial. It is a precious gift you may give yourself. Flow with it. Explore each nuance. Imprint it upon your long-term memory sectors. There it will reside, accessible any time you need.

Embrace this blissful feeling of being loved and deeply cherished, as if you were the only child in the world, for in the eyes of Creator, you are.

Bask in appreciation for the enormous gift your angels have shared with you today.

Glory in the joy of simply being.

Revel in this magnificent experience. No cares or worries. You're completely at peace.

If you hear whispers from your angels, focus your attention upon them. Allow whatever they want to share to flow effortlessly into your consciousness.

Allow them to gently stroke the neural pathways of your brain, smoothing out any damaged or distorted bits, restoring them to pristine condition. You may feel the reverberations of their ministrations or not. Either is perfect.

Allow, relax, breathe. You are safely and deeply connected to your incredible team, who are your biggest cheerleaders and help mates. They do it all with nary a complaint. It is their joy and privilege to do so. You are **THEIR** reason for being. They were created just for you!

And now, just when you think things couldn't feel any more incredible, Creator approaches to scoop you up to be cradled in the arms of the most unfathomable love you've ever felt.

Your tiny heart could nearly burst with joy, but it won't — because Creator's got you.

Memorize every tiny detail of this experience. It will sustain you when you're weary and careworn. Like a shot of adrenaline, you can access it when the need arises to recapture this exquisite feeling of perfect beingness. You may return to this space to draw upon the well of Creation any time you like.

Today is your heightened awareness day. The moment, when like a child learning to walk, you reach out and take the outstretched hand that provides confidence and stability. A new level of development. Today is that magnified a thousandfold (or more), but who's counting? (God Wink.)

Now, as if a babe arising from deep slumber, stretch your arms and legs. Allow the blood to flow freely. Bring your awareness back to your breathing. Take your time and when you're ready, open your eyes.

Take a couple of deep breaths as you return to third-dimensional awareness. Then spend a moment or two thanking all that is for this profound experiential journey. For, in the giving of thanks, you will anchor the experience into present reality.

Amen.

SPIRITUAL RENEWAL & CLEANSING

*S*it back, close your eyes, and take a couple of deep cleansing breaths. Then return to your normal breathing pattern.

Focus on each breath as you inhale, hold, and then exhale.

If you find that your thoughts start to stray, that's okay, just go back to focusing on your breathing. It's all good, no stress, no strain. Just allow every care and woe to fall away.

Feel the energy rising as you're lifted up to connect with the *Akashic* realm. With your eyes still closed, you find yourself standing in a park-like setting.

The sun shines warmly upon you. The grass is brilliant green. It feels wonderful, like a cushion under your bare feet. Wiggle your toes and revel in that lovely feeling of cushiony grass. Maybe it tickles you as it pops up between your toes.

There's a lovely, gentle breeze caressing your face. You lean back and gaze up at the sky. As you do that, your mouth reflexively opens wide and you shift into a state of receiving.

From high above, a viscous, liquid energy — *vital force energy* — begins pouring down into your throat, glug, glug, glug...

Pouring down and down, continuing for some time, filling you up until you're overflowing.

Vital force energy is coming out of your eyes, your nose, your ears. It's everywhere! Abundance... so much abundance that your vessel cannot contain it all.

Now, you may think being filled to overflowing is wasteful. No, My Dear. That is lack mentality. Let it go.

The universe is abundant. There's an unceasing flow of *vital force energy* available to you always.

It is you who cuts it off during times of panic and fear. In those moments, when you realize what has happened, stop, breathe, relax, and allow the energy to move freely once more.

Everything you need is available to you. It always was. You just couldn't see it in a state of panic; because when you focus upon fear and panic, what you get is more fear and panic.

Notice the viscous liquid is now even on the bottoms of your feet. Now that you've noticed, you realize it feels quite sticky and uncomfortable.

So, you walk over to a lovely wooden bench sitting under a massive maple tree.

Sitting down on the bench, you contemplate your sticky feet, which are now clumped with bits of grass and dirt from your short walk. You decide to ignore that for the moment, because you're excited to see what comes next.

While sitting quietly on your bench, you notice a figure approaching. It may be an angel, a guide, or someone else (I saw Jesus). Don't worry if you can't see their features clearly, that's not important.

Simply accept and allow them to appear as they choose, because they have come to assist you.

In fact, they have come to wash your feet. This wonderful, beneficent presence carefully removes the clumps and sticky substance; thoroughly cleansing all traces from your feet.

You sit and observe, in a state of deep appreciation, as you now understand: this is about more than your feet.

It's about washing away old trauma. Trauma that has adhered to your energy body and was slowing your progress. Realization dawns. This is a spiritual renewal and cleansing, performed with a great deal of love and care as layer upon layer is removed.

When your feet are completely cleaned, out comes a big, fluffy towel to thoroughly dry them. You experience a feeling of being deeply loved and pampered.

Sit back and allow yourself to be ministered to without protesting; because *a part of your spiritual growth is learning to gratefully accept without objection.*

After the cleansing, you and your friend sit together on the bench, contemplating life. From this perspective in the *Akasha*, you're able to look down and observe humanity hustling and bustling to and fro.

Your cleansing bestowed upon you greater clarity and vision. While looking down at those people, you wonder: "Why are they all in such a hurry? Don't they realize they create more angst for themselves when they engage with that frenetic energy? It's like saying to the Universe, *yes, I want more chaos and strife.*

You will remember this understanding in the days to come as your ruminations turn towards your own life experience.

You now realize that *you* are the conductor of your train. The speed at which you travel is up to you. You realize it might be wise to adjust your throttle down a notch or two so that you might enjoy the scenery along the way. Because when you're whizzing along at full speed, you miss the delights, not to mention the breadcrumbs, your angels have carefully set out for you.

No wonder you sometimes feel like your head is spinning. Your poor eyes haven't had a chance to clearly focus upon the sights at this speed. With your eyes still closed, hold your hand up in front of your face. Look at it. Really see it, like you've never seen it before.

Isn't it a marvel the way it's constructed? The way it functions. The strength and dexterity for something relatively small. It serves a mighty big purpose.

How about some appreciation for that hand — and the other one too? Appreciation of your entire body, for that matter. It's a marvel in function and design, yet most of the time, you take it for granted. When you're doing those gratitude affirmations and journals, how about some love for your amazing hands, your body, and yourself?

You are a marvel. Sure, Creator crafted all the parts and the interior design, but it is *you* who tested, tweaked, and modified, to evolve into the miraculous creation you are today, right now in this moment.

You rarely give yourself credit for the wisdom, the lessons, or the courage in venturing out of your comfort zone.

Those pivotal moments in your journey that cause you to shift into recognizing and acting upon Divine guidance are to be celebrated.

The lessons you've learned, the way you've transformed lumps of coal into sparkling diamonds, are all reasons to celebrate you.

Take that lesson and leave the rest. It served its purpose. Let it go. There are many wonderful adventures yet to come. Do not allow yourself to be tethered to past events (which you call mistakes), that will lead to bringing more of the same into your experience.

Why would you do that? Release them. Allow new and exciting experiences to flow in. Recapture the joy, wonder, and delight that you felt as a child. That is your natural state of being. *That is the state of flowing.*

Find something to delight in and allow it to expand. There's always something. It's in that deliberate *reaching for a feeling* state when you throw the doors wide open for more and better.

What you focus upon expands. Do you want to focus upon an ouchy, skinned knee, or do you want to focus upon all the ways that you're blessed?

Focus upon blessings, and you will have more blessings to focus upon. That is the wise choice of an empowered soul.

More you ask? Yes, there's always more. For now, pause, reflect, allow your awareness of how richly blessed you are to expand, and the blessings to multiply as surely as little rabbits will.

Fertility... that's a topic for another day. Go in peace and never forget: you are forever and always wrapped in the loving arms of Divine Creator, for that is how very precious you are.

Over and out...

PEACE & CALM FOR EVERYONE

*C*oming down from the heavens above is a blazing, fiery, tangerine orange ball.

It's a massive burst of Divine love light that's now sinking gently into your crown chakra. As it enters your body and moves down through your brain, you might feel a tingling sensation.

As the ball lights you up from the inside out, it energizes and fills you with more love, light, faith, and trust to support you through the uncomfortable days whilst humanity expands and evolves.

Feel that fiery ball crackling as it moves down into your heart chakra, where it feels like a great big bear hug as you're held tightly to the bosom of Divine. A love like nothing you've ever felt. Warms you, fills you with peace and love for all of humanity, the peace that passes understanding that is pure bliss.

Now the ball is moving down into your solar plexus. It's powering up your engines in the most amazing way so that you feel on fire, rarin' to go. You're ready to face whatever dragons are in your path, with peace and love.

You now know, to the very core of your being, that you *can* overcome any obstacle in your path.

The fiery ball next moves down to your sacral chakra, your seat of abundance, wealth, sexuality, what makes you who you are. It lights you up like a pinball machine so that you'll manifest that which you desire more rapidly.

Know that is part of who you are, how you were designed to be. It will all come forth when you are in this state of peace, love, and confidence. The truth of Divine.

The fire ball is on the move again as it sinks into your root chakra. The very essence of you. Lighting you up still more in a gentle, loving way. This time, causing you to levitate. You feel so light, loved and completely at peace.

More bliss for you, and emanating from you, to the world, so that all who come in contact with you will also feel it. They'll know you've got something special to share, and they'll be magnetically drawn to you, eager to hear your blessed message.

With that, the golden orange ball sinks all the way down, exiting your body, and gently sinking into Mother Earth. You share this experience with her, because you're deeply connected to Gaia, who supports and nurtures you.

You're now safely and securely grounded between Earth and Divine. You're an empowered warrior, ready to go out into your day to face any challenge in faith and confidence, knowing that you have all you need within you.

You have that Divine power within you. That essence remains there. Helping you have more confidence, faith, and trust in your own ability to stand and face whatever comes in peace and love.

And so it is.

ENCOUNTER WITH A STAR

*A*s you begin this meditation, take a moment to set your intention to send love, peace, healing, and calm to the Earth and all her inhabitants.

Then, take a couple of deep breaths. Allow your body to relax back into your chair. Close your eyes and tune into your body.

Where is it tight? Where is there heaviness? As you notice, feel your tension slipping away as you comfortably settle into a deeply relaxed state.

Now with your eyes still closed, look around at your surroundings.

What do you notice? Are you on the beach? Are you in the mountains? Are you in your home? Or, maybe a beautiful pasture?

Wherever you are is perfect, and you can allow that scene to morph along the way.

Breathe in all of the aromas waiting there for your enjoyment. If there's sun, feel the sunshine warming your upturned face. Be one with nature. Feel your heartbeat synchronizing with the heartbeat of Gaia.

Notice how your feet feel upon the ground. Perhaps you feel a little tingle as you connect. Feel the love she sends up to you. The warmth, nourishment, the care.

And now, look up. Notice far, far above what looks like a bright, gleaming Star, twinkling in the sky.

As you marvel at the beauty of this incredible Star, more magnificent than any you've seen before, notice it twinkles, as if it's winking at you.

Yes, the Star is acknowledging your presence! That's how important you are, Beautiful Soul, that the Star is taking time to acknowledge your presence.

As you process this astonishing realization, a long, beautiful white arm reaches out to you from the Star.

An arm and hand descending towards you, until the hand is gently cupping your head. You might feel tingling, or even a jolt as the energy of the Star connects with your body.

Can you feel the warmth buzzing through your brain? What do suppose the Star has to share with you today?

Now the tingling and buzzing move down your body, past your face, your neck, your shoulders… tingling, tingling all the way.

This Star is infusing *you* with its vital life force. You are being a lit up and energized by magical, Star energy.

The tingling/buzzing continues moving down your torso, over your hips and legs, past your ankles, through your feet and right into the ground, connecting with Mother Earth.

There you are, suspended between a Star and the Earth. You are now lit by Stardust. Take a moment to notice the tingles moving through your entire body.

And now, this beautiful Star has a message to share. She wants you to know that you *can* have peace, calm, healing, and love — in this moment — and in every moment.

It's a choice. No matter what goes on in the world, you Beautiful Soul, have the power to create this moment of reality for yourself in every moment. Whenever you feel fizzy, staticky, disruptive, energy intruding upon your peace and calm demeanor, return to this moment of connection with your special Star and the Earth. Then allow yourself to be filled once more with peace, calm, healing, and love.

This glorious infusion is a gift to you from the beautiful Star, Creator, and Mother Earth. It's as if they are holding you while simultaneously infusing you with the light and love of the Universe.

Yes, it is that vast, yours for the asking, and even more importantly, for the receiving. Because the truth is, this gift was always available to you. All you needed to do was receive it.

As the creator of your reality, you choose when (or if), to receive a peace, calm, healing, love infusion. Simply ask, wait in the moment, then receive. It will always come when you ask.

If you can imagine it, you can ask for it. Then watch what happens to your world.

Now, filled to overflowing, allow infusion energy to exude from your body to flow into the world. There it will intersect with others who are in discord, and most certainly not at peace.

They may choose to receive or not. Either is fine, because they, like you, are sovereign over their soul and journey. You, Dear Beautiful Soul, only need send it out with love to connect with whomever chooses to receive.

The more often you do that, the greater the power will grow. Each time it will touch more souls. Each time more souls will receive.

You will witness a wave of peace, calm, healing, and love flowing across the entire earth.

A sea change is coming and you are a part of it — if you choose to be. Your angels invite you on this peaceful journey. Know that they will be with you each step of the way, helping you through the sticky parts, loving and laughing with you through the smooth, joyful parts.

Just enjoy the journey, because that's why you're here. It's all about your journey and what you choose to make of it. Whatever is present in your life today that is not pleasing to you, know that it's there because you chose it. And you can choose to release it, anytime. Let it go.

Obligation, responsibility, you do not have to take them on — unless you choose — no matter what anyone tells you.

Because, from your soul's karmic perspective, choosing to take on all of that responsibility is creating the karma of more responsibility.

That's wonderful if it's responsibility that you enjoy, but if it's obligatory responsibility, that represents a burden which negatively impacts your soul journey. Know that you can choose to release it and it's in your soul's best interest to do so.

As you journey this world, notice the fruitful bounty. When you choose, only choose the juiciest, most delicious.

Picture yourself in a big apple orchard: your hand reaches up to pluck a beautiful apple from the tree. You're not going to choose one that's bruised, or wormy. You're going to choose the best apple on that tree, and that is perfect, as it should be.

Know that your entire soul journey can be that way, always choosing the very best.

It's what your creator wants for you and it's what your soul wants. When you make it your practice to choose and enjoy the very best, you'll have more to share with the world.

And so it is.

Take a couple of deep breaths. Wiggle your fingers and toes. Then come back to us from that beautiful place that you journeyed to. Remember what you've experienced and know that you can experience it again anytime you like.

THE UNDERPINNINGS OF WELLBEING

*U*nfolding before you is a scene of whiteness, with tiny silver sparkles, like lightly applied glitter. Now, comes a splash of royal blue running down slowly, covering the wall.

In front of the now blue wall appears a red veil of translucent fabric. Bright red. The veil stands between you and the blue wall, gently floating in a light breeze. Next, a yellow veil appears to the right of the red. This veil is thicker and less translucent.

Now the bigger picture comes into view. You're inside a cabana located on a gorgeous white-sand beach.

You walk out, barefoot, onto the sand. It's hot on your feet, but cool when your foot sinks down with each step. You walk towards the water, a glorious Caribbean blue lit by bright sunlight. There's a lovely breeze, and the temperature is perfection.

You walk down to where the waves meet the sand and sit down, just out of reach of the water. You revel in the peacefulness as you focus on the waves lapping the shore.

Looking up, you see three seagulls flying over the water, occasionally calling out. They seem to be flying in some sort of circular pattern. Round and round, looking at the water and only occasionally looking up. Something they see or sense has their rapt attention.

You notice a dark shape in the water. Just then, one of the gulls dives down for a closer look. In a split second, an orca whale bursts through the water, leaping high into the air, snatching the gull in mid-flight.

Orca re-enters the water with a splash and a satisfied crunch. That gull is quite tasty and has momentarily quelled her case of the munchies. With her urge satiated, she lazily swims back towards deeper water.

You are left sitting, mouth agape in astonishment, wondering how feathers and a whale's digestive system get along.

After a few more moments, you stand up, dust yourself off, and begin walking north along the beach, occasionally stopping to pick up an interesting shell. Soon you have a pocketful in your billowing, white gauzy pants.

As you approach the end of the beach, there are wooden stairs, with a handrail, leading up towards a beach house. There's a lovely deck with lots of big windows on the beach side. Not terribly ornate, but a very comfortable house. The deck doors are open and the breeze is blowing the curtains lightly about.

You can see the kitchen from the deck and, finding yourself famished, begin planning what to make for dinner. You decide on a big salad with vinaigrette dressing. For an appetizer, mozzarella slices with tomato and basil, drizzled with extra-virgin olive oil, accompanied by a nice white wine. For dessert, something light like lemon bars.

Sounds perfect and you smile in anticipation of sitting down to such a lovely meal. Maybe you'll even add some zucchini slices, coated in coconut oil and grilled. That would make a nice accompaniment.

As you look around at the cozy cottage, and salivate in anticipation over the meal you've planned, realization dawns that this is truly living in well being.

Happy with the simple pleasures, your needs are met, living near and in harmony with nature, enjoying some pleasant background music and the company of someone whose conversation is intelligent and interesting.

It's like a little cocoon apart from the chaos of the daily grind. With a deep breath, you inhale the vital spark of life that surrounds you.

You spend some moments basking in appreciation for this vision of abundant living. Soaking in the message that this is the way life is meant to be lived. It's important that you carve out these moments to maintain sanity in an often insane world.

Being a compassionate soul, your mind turns to those who do not have such luxuries and inquire of your angels: "What would you say to them?"

You're immediately reminded that everyone has the ability to have these luxuries in their meditations. They can create amazing, peaceful realms in visions and happily inhabit them for short periods of time. The visions are as real as you want them to be.

Everyone, unless they are prisoners, has the ability to go out and find places in nature to soak up the vital, energetic spark of life. It costs nothing and is available 24/7.

Even if it's just a potted plant, you can find something living and spend time communing with the energy it produces. While you are soaking up energy from the plant, you are, in turn, feeding that plant with each exhale.

It is perfection! An endless cycle of cooperation and life-giving energy, feeding you — body and soul. Nourishing you physically and spiritually. An amazing, grand design of genius proportion.

The intelligence required to put together such disparate pieces, creating a whole of this magnitude, is unfathomable. Incredibly, you are a part of that intelligence!

Like pebbles that break off from a larger whole, distinct and individual, yet you still contain pieces, DNA even, of the originator and add your experiences to form who you are at this time and place. It is a marvel! And when your expansion and exploration has concluded, you will return to the origination and become part of the whole once more, contributing your individuality, making the whole greater than the sum of its parts. Now that's a heady concept!

As this truth and knowledge seeps into your psyche, you're momentarily overwhelmed at the magnitude. It's not the light meal you planned, instead, it's a seven-course feast, and you're feeling stuffed to the gills (figuratively speaking).

Spent, you collapse onto the overstuffed sofa. It's like the welcoming feel of sinking into the softest pillows you can imagine. Deliciously luxurious!

When you catch your breath, you decide that a soak in the hot tub (which you've just added to your vision), is just the thing.

Sinking into the lovely water, you heave a deep sigh of release. Sitting there in the water is the perfect place to reflect upon the lesson you've just been given as you allow it to assimilate into your being. Thoughts are buzzing in your head like a hive of bees.

Yes, this is good.

Now, hear the message from your angels: Pause to allow this lesson to integrate deeply into your psyche. Rest and restore your energetic supply, then go out into the world and interact using this new understanding.

Notice the changes. Do people react to you differently? Do you react to them differently? What new perceptions come? Do the colors you encounter seem brighter? Are things that used to be difficult suddenly easier? Do you find new inspirations coming easier? Do you have a sense of knowing certain things that you didn't have before? Has your zest for life increased? Are you finding it easier to remain in a state of wellbeing?

That is the ultimate goal. Has your score increased on that front? If it has not, then stop and reevaluate.

Are you incorporating the new lessons you've learned, or have you fallen back into old non-productive habits?

In the beginning, you may find that you must be vigilant lest you fall into that trap. You are worth the effort of living fully in your new understanding of who you are and your place in the universe. It's a gift you can give to yourself, but only *you* can make it happen. No one else can do it for you.

Are you hesitating? Why? What are you afraid of? Did you not ask for a better life? What is stopping you from stepping into your new reality? Are you blocked?

We are here ready and willing to help with the blocks and the fears. We are your team. We stand at your beck and call. We have nothing more important to do than attend to your needs. All you must do is ask and it will be given. When it is given, *take* it.

This is your birthright. You were meant to thrive and live in a state of abundance and well being. We will *never* give up on you.

No matter how many times you fall, we will always be here to help you up and to move forward. Let us do our job *please!*

Do you understand now just how much you are loved and how important you are? Yes, little old you! Come running into our loving embrace and allow us to guide you onto the path of your true destiny. We eagerly await.

. . .

With love, Your Akashic Team

Why this message now? Because, there are too few who actually hear and understand this truth. We will keep broadcasting for as long as necessary to reach you. You are *that* important. When you're ready, just say the word. We'll be there. (Cue Michael Jackson singing: *I'll Be There*. Written by Berry Gordy, et al. 1970)

WEARING THE MANTLE OF AN AWAKENED SOUL

*A*s the year is winding down, you're presented with an opportunity for introspection and planning for the new year ahead.

How do you feel about the preceding eleven months? Did you accomplish what you had hoped?

Are you satisfied with your results? What lessons did you learn? How will you use those lessons to make next year even better?

With those questions in mind, let's begin the meditation.

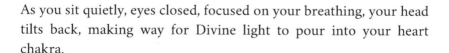

As you sit quietly, eyes closed, focused on your breathing, your head tilts back, making way for Divine light to pour into your heart chakra.

Your body is being filled with incredible warmth and well being. A very auspicious beginning indeed.

When you're filled to overflowing, the light filters down, deep into the earth, causing your body to undulate from the powerful waves of energy. It's almost balletic and very rhythmic.

You're making music with the Divine. What a wonderful feeling! You dance around like a ballerina en pointe in a little pink tutu.

That visual causes you to giggle at the absurdity. You think: *this physical body is not congruent with that sort of movement.*

Your angels whisper in response: *But your soul is.*

Ah, you stand corrected.

The ballerina version of you then whirls and twirls out of sight.

The doors to your *Records* open wide, revealing a glorious spring day. Everything fresh, clean, and vibrant.

As you step inside, you're greeted with the fragrance of daffodils, and a perfect, gentle breeze caressing your face.

You exhale deeply, releasing all concerns which are washed away instantly by the vision and energetic frequency of the *Akasha*.

You feel so wonderful that you burst into song: *Oh what a beautiful morning, oh what a beautiful day, I've got a beautiful feeling everything's going my way.* (From the Broadway musical Oklahoma.)

That song elicits sparkling, pure energy, exactly the frequency of magnificent manifestations. A feast for the senses. Your body can't help but feel lighter and move rhythmically along. This is bliss. So powerful that movement is *required.*

When the Divine puts on such a show, you simply must respond, it's encoded in your DNA.

Allow it to bring you out of your daily routine. Allow it to inspire you to new experiences. Allow yourself to step into this energetic pool of bliss.

That's the trouble with your world *Grasshopper*, not enough allowing, not enough bliss. Everyone all caught up in their own agendas. Busy, busy, busy, running about like chickens with their heads cut off. So much drama. Why? Do you not make the connection that it draws you in the opposite direction from whence you intended? Do you not see how it derails your plans?

Stop hey, what's that sound? Everybody look what's going round. (Buffalo Springfield, For What It's Worth, 1966.)

It's a distraction! You *don't* have to respond to every distraction that comes along. Do you allow a pesky gnat buzzing about your head to derail you? Of course not because you realize it is temporary and unimportant. Why then do you allow distractions that have nothing to do with *you* to completely derail your plans?

Were those plans not so very important after all? It's an important consideration. What *is* really important to you? What do you value? Once you get clear on those questions, consider whether that's where you're putting your energy and focus. If not, maybe you should.

You get to decide what's important and how you spend your time, we only want to help you see that very often what you intend and what you actually *do* are very different.

Bring more awareness to your daily life. Get off the treadmill of eat/sleep/work. That is not what you came to the planet to experience.

Chop chop, **WAKE UP!**

You are missing from your own life. You are *not* an automaton. You are a living, breathing, feeling, thinking being. Isn't it time you exercised your rights and stepped into living rather than existing? My child, you are missing out on the exquisite experience that you came here to have.

It's all well and good to climb up on the carousel and take a ride occasionally. It's a different matter entirely to spend your whole life there. Step off and step into awareness of who you really are. Allow yourself to feel *everything*.

Don't slip into the trap of numbness to escape the unpleasant parts of your existence. Do something about it! Take some new action. Make a new choice. Going numb is being stagnant. Allow yourself to feel so that you can discern what you *don't* want and leave it behind.

It takes courage to wear the Mantle of an Awakened Soul. You will at times see and feel things that are not pretty. Nevertheless, it's reality. Once you see it, then you get to choose what you do about it.

We promise that even in those times when you believe there's no choice, there *always* is. Just do something different. Get the energy flowing and watch for bread crumbs from your angels. We'll be right there with you. We *are* even now. Tune into our presence. Allow us to assist. You don't have to do this alone. That is a choice, but from our perspective, a very unwise one.

Why would you pilot a yacht yourself, when you have an entire crew at your disposal? That crew will come in mighty handy when you encounter rough seas, which you most assuredly will. It's polarity you see. Calm/rough. Both have their place.

Too much calm and you have stagnation, which ultimately becomes death. Too much rough keeps you in survival mode, where nothing gets accomplished — except surviving — and for what? Neither is desirable. Balance is what you're trying to achieve.

It's a whole lot easier to maintain balance when you can see the big picture and allow others to help you *get by with a little help from your friends. Gonna try with a little help from your friends.* (With A Little Help From My Friends, Joe Cocker, 1969)

The world is your playground. You've lost track of that by choosing to become laden down with responsibilities.

You are magnificent manifestors, every one of you. It's encoded within you. Allow it to come out and be expressed once more.

We are not saying you shouldn't work, however there is work, and there is work. When you do what you love it isn't really work, is it?

How can you incorporate more joy into what you do so that it will feed your soul, uplift your energy, open your awareness to the possibilities that are even now right in front of you?

Ask for what you *really* want. Allow us to help you manifest something even better than you thought to ask for.

Allow is a big part of the answer you've been seeking. *Because you have free choice, you are free to block your own manifestations,* and some of you have gotten quite good at it.

Stop allowing others to tell you who you are and what you *should* do. Those are *their* rules, not yours. *You* get to create rules that work for you.

Question everything! Accepting someone else's version of truth has *never* served you. Open your eyes. Use your gifts to see with clarity and vision.

See the world as you would have it be. Then move towards that beautiful vision and watch for the metaphorical stepping stones that will be laid out before you to make the journey easier.

Divine never said it had to be hard. That is a human invention and comes from limited thinking.

Time to climb up out of that box. Better yet, knock the walls down! You, Beautiful Soul, were not created to live in a box — most especially not one designed by someone else.

Lift up your eyes to the vision of what you intend and then get moving. The tiniest baby steps are perfectly fine. It's just important to move.

Inertia is not your friend. It will pull you right off course and drag you down into despair if you let it. Please don't. You have important things to do.

There's a purpose and plan to this incarnation that you designed before you were born into this skin suit. Reconnect with that purpose. Meditation is one way, there are others. Choose what works best for you. Get help if you need it.

There is so much joy, wonder and delight just waiting for you around the bend, so what are you waiting for? Life is meant to be a voyage of discovery so get up and roll it along. (*A Marshmallow World*, Carl Sigman & Peter DeRose, 1949, popularized by Dean Martin.)

We say Ye Hallelujah and Amen.

RECOVERING LOST PARTS
OF SELF

a grounding pillar of light descends from above, like a heat-seeking missile, blasting through your crown chakra, down your body and into the earth until it reaches magma.

As you process this unusual grounding, the purpose becomes clear. It's an extra-strength grounding cord which acts as a secure anchor. Although, this grounding cord has a flexible feel, like a huge rubber band.

The cord weaves through the earth, tying off little bows, swirling into decorative script flourishes — almost like lacing a shoe, until finally with a sigh of satisfaction, ceases movement.

There's stillness. All activity has ceased. As if life itself is at a standstill.

The stillness is shortly replaced by a soft, swaying feel as if you're a sapling, gently moved by the breeze. The breeze causes your leaves to flutter, and you to sway to and fro. You are safe. Deeply grounded betwixt and between Creator and Mother Earth.

Womb... Bloom... Tomb... rinse, repeat, and so it goes.

You spring forth from the womb, bursting upon a world that is familiar, and yet at the same time, new. Like an incredibly vivid dream. Until you open your eyes, and the dream is swiftly replaced with new experiences.

All that remains of the once vivid dream are fragments, disjointed bits, and yet a familiarness occasionally creeps in. Briefly flitting across the movie screen of your mind.

You call that deja vu. It is actually memory, an opportunity to recover those forgotten memories. Like pulling the string on a roll of lifesavers, sweetness and variety await inside.

These opportunities to recapture lost bits of yourself appear periodically in your life. Should you recognize them, and invite more detail to return to your consciousness, you would find that more follow.

However, until now, you've been distracted by other concerns and the opportunity quickly vanishes. These opportunities are more fragile than butterfly wings.

That is why until recent times they have remained largely unavailable. However, now that you have ascended to a higher vibration, those memories are within reach. All you need do is pause when they appear. Wait in that quiet space and allow. Coax them forward, nurturing the spark of memory.

Allow it to grow into a glowing ember, revealing more of who you have been, and lessons you have learned. Rich experiences from your historical archive. It's yours and you may access it as you choose.

It will take some practice to develop your own technique of coaxing them forth. It may take substantial effort. That is not to say you need stress and strain. Far from it. These things cannot be forced, for that results in the memory receding, like a turtle into its shell, unreachable. It's reflexive, you see.

Float into allowing. Only then will it return as a full-fledged memory, once more restored to you.

Is that a delightful thought, my child? Then intend it and allow it to manifest in your life. After all, it is recorded in your soul's DNA, it is a part of you. These are powerful memory connections that left an imprint upon you. That is why they show up in an accessible form. Now that you understand what these events are, formulate a plan.

How will you trigger a response to recover those fleeting wisps of memory next time?

Perhaps journal about it. For in the focus time during journaling, you will effortlessly draw near to the fragment of memory.

As you practice and focus, you will find it gets easier and faster to bring a memory into focus. Then you can preserve it in some fashion, adding it to your collection, forming the sections of your life's tapestry.

Then bask in appreciation for the wonder that is you. Basking energy paves the way for more memories to come forth.

Focus, basking, allowing, those are all vital to the process of rediscovering the you that was.

As you reconstruct what was, more pieces will appear, faster and faster, until one day you realize that you have assembled a significant portion of your story. You will feel more *you-er* than you. As if you've grown into shoes that were only recently too large.

It is a reconnection at the fifth dimensional level. It will feel enormous, like nothing you've ever felt before.

Massive transformation.

More clarity blooms, nearly instantaneously. It is a marvel! *This* is what you've been waiting for highly conscious soul.

This is what it means to meet your soul. That part of you that you've previously only glimpsed in passing. Elusive, and ethereal, always seeming just out of reach. The you that drifts away between the brief moment when you awaken and when you open your eyes.

Reaching this place is a massive milestone. It portends faster and even more deeply satisfying progress on your journey. Savor it. For once you pass this milestone, you will never recapture that awakening experience and it is *delicious*.

Each of these milestones are different and thrilling in their own way, however, this one is special.

This one is your opportunity to open the door to retaining the truth of who you are, so that in your *next* incarnation you'll come from the womb to remain in an awakened state.

Imagine the depth of experience that lifetime, and future ones, will offer when you come to this third dimensional experience with a massive head start. The world is your oyster.

And with all that being said, dear one, should you not reach this milestone in the present incarnation, we promise you will in a future one. There is no rush. Everything is unfolding in divine timing. Rejoice and be glad in it, for today is a new day and there is more potential each new day than there was in the previous. You are becoming more than you were. One day closer to who you will be. It is a beautiful sight to behold.

Whilst you journey ever forward, please do not neglect your inner child. Ensure that you factor in a play quotient.

Just like meditation, sometimes mere minutes are all that is needed. Jump in a mud puddle from time to time. Play hopscotch. Take a detour through a playground, and linger there, perhaps taking a turn on the merry go round, or a quick trip down the slide. Soar towards the sky on a swing.

Whatever brings you delight or makes you giggle. There is far too little giggling happening in your world. Bring it back. Make it a part of your day. Search for opportunities to share it with others.

Oh yes, share it with others, for in those moments you make greater progress towards reconnecting with your authentic self than years of diligent study might produce.

Are you getting the picture? Your journey isn't about working hard or struggling. Your soul is ready to soar, not be harnessed to a millstone. So skip on out into the world and keep an eye out for playful interludes.

This is your angel team signing off for now. Over and out.

TO THE OUTER LIMITS
AND BACK

This meditative journey is like none other that I have channeled. It's a trip to the outer limits that at times might feel like the Twilight Zone.

A powerful lesson on life and death transitions. Not your everyday meditation.

Ominous dark skies, fear so palpable you can smell it on the air. Chaos and confusion all around. A serious threat to your well being and soul journey. However, you Dear One, need not be a part of that madness.

Let us take you on a strange and wonderful journey to see the bigger picture, which will hopefully ease your mind and allow you to maintain your well being and a peaceful outlook no matter what is happening around you.

Close your eyes, take some deep cleansing breaths. Allow yourself to release all the cares and woes that invade your peace as you move into a normal breathing pattern.

Know that you are safe and loved. Nothing can harm you in this space. While some of the imagery may be unusual, that it is purposeful and serves to convey an important message that you need to hear at this time as you prepare for what is yet to come.

Breathe, relax, and allow yourself to float effortlessly through this meditational journey, firmly ensconced in the arms of your angels, safe and loved.

You may see and feel the angels, or you may not, either is perfect.

The first image you see forming out of a wall of blackness is that of a hand holding a silver pistol. First cocking, and then pulling the trigger at very close range.

As the gun fires, you can see the bullet traveling towards you as if in slow motion with a trailing puff of smoke left behind. You stand motionless, transfixed, feeling no fear, just curiosity as to what is behind this strange image.

You continue hearing the reverberations of the shot long past the time of actually seeing it fire. Almost like a crack of lightning followed by thunder, but you feel nothing, like being frozen in time. The bullet never reached you or your angels pulled you out of your body before you felt the impact. No matter which. The important thing to notice is that your angels never wavered and were with you throughout.

As you process this experience, focus on being present. Breathe in and out. Let your consciousness expand, allowing for greater insights and understanding. Moving past your daily level of being-ness into a higher vibrational frequency, reaching for the stars and beyond.

You are a limitless being. As the Creator of your reality, you are free to expand upon present circumstances, as you allow for the wisdom of the Universe to gently boop you on the nose, inviting you to come and play. Oh what adventures you will have in this limitless state of being.

Should you find yourself struggling to move beyond the limiting space of present reality, call upon your team to inspire and spark your imagination. If you can think it you can be it.

Do not judge the experience, simply allow it to unfold.

Let loose of limitation. Spread your arms and fly. Rise up into the atmosphere, soar above the treetops like a magnificent bird. Feel the power and wonder of soaring high above the daily grind. Marvel at your enhanced perspective. You can easily dip down to get a better look at anything that captures your attention and you can soar back up, flying above the clouds should you desire.

Remembering that you are limitless, you may fly even higher moving out of Earth's gravitational pull into outer space. You needn't worry about such things as reentry burns or breaking through the atmosphere because you are creating this story and such obstacles need not be part of it. That bears repeating: **YOU** are creating your story so make it a good one!

Want to explore other planets? They are but a thought away. Want to go further into another galaxy? You can do that too. For it is your consciousness, not your third-dimensional self that is taking this journey.

If you know that you originated on another planet you may visit that planet to get a first-hand experience of what it and the inhabitants look like. Don't question or judge the experience simply flow with it.

Explore, learn about their society, how they spend their time, what their interests are. What does their family life look like? What's important to them? Does it feel familiar? Perhaps you're getting flashbacks of former lives when you lived here. Soak it all in being very present in the moment so that you'll remember.

Want to visit other planets? You can do that too.

Perhaps you'd like to explore your Akashic archive to learn more about yourself. While there you may choose to spend time with departed loved ones or perhaps historical personalities about whom you'd like to know more. Galileo springs to mind.

You may call upon anyone you like. Most will be quite willing to come. Some will not because it is after all, their choice. They may be occupied with other matters and simply not available. Do not take it personally. You can ask for them another time.

Now into your field of vision comes a bright orange/yellow, like the sun. It's huge and pervasive. As you gaze and wonder what this means it occurs to you that it looks like an egg yolk seen from the inside, from the vantage point of an embryo, looking out at the world through the viscous liquid of yolk, watching the world grow smaller as you grow larger.

You notice a feeling of being cramped and confined then with a burst of energy throw your arms wide, stretching your body as you burst through the confinement container, breaking through to a much larger world.

You're now taking your first breaths in the outside world, choking a bit as your lungs are cleared of the life-giving liquid that has sustained you since you were merely a speck.

Things are changing rapidly now. New sights, sounds and sensations. So much to learn. You soak it up voraciously for this is why you were born, to have third-dimensional experiences that are exquisitely visceral. You're in this messy life up to your elbows rather than floating above observing as consciousness.

While that is a marvelous experience, there's a feeling of disconnection as you are presently watching yourself from the outside looking in.

Whilst you're in a third-dimensional body, life is very real, messy, fun, exciting, sometimes terrifying yet even that is exhilarating as you find new ways to experience life.

That scene has now been replaced with one of milky whiteness everywhere, thick and viscous. Stark, and without contrast, it feels a bit cloying, suffocating even.

There's no relief from the endless whiteness.

Recognition dawns. This is the stage of existence coming directly after death of the physical body. Of course it stands in stark contrast to life.

This place functions like a docking station where you transition from one reality to another. It's a purifying, cleansing process that occurs before emerging back into pure consciousness.

There's a feeling of heaviness in your heart chakra as you disconnect from the threads of third-dimensional living. Many attachments to be released. The sensation of lungs filling with air, and beating heart, now mere echoes, are slipping away as you further adjust to leaving behind another third-dimensional body.

You notice feeling an expansiveness now that your life force is no longer encapsulated in a third-dimensional container.

Flashes of memories pass by then quickly fade as you reconnect with a cumulative data bank of past-lives. They flood in, swirling around together, reorganizing into the new you of this present reality.

This is what you might call the limbo portion of your journey. It can be uncomfortable and require some period of adjustment. The longer the third-dimensional life, the longer it can take to reorient.

After being in this white viscosity reality for a while, it becomes normal and comfortable. Vaguely reminiscent of being in the egg yolk that you experienced earlier. You relax and settle in allowing yourself to just be.

It strikes you that your existence is made up of different states of beingness. You transition from one to another in an ongoing endless cycle, fully engaged in each stage along the way. Your perception of reality shifting as you go. Initially feeling disoriented, then moving into curiosity, before full acceptance, and once more becoming comfortable with your present phase.

While it would seem that having been through this process many times before, no adjustment time would be needed, each time you cycle through you are at a different stage of soul evolution, so it's never exactly the same. This is also a part of learning, growing, and consciousness expansion.

It is perfectly normal to feel resistance to this sort of change as the transitions can sometimes be quite abrupt when you find yourself unceremoniously awakening into what might feel like an episode of the *Twilight Zone*. That feeling is fleeting and you quickly adjust each and every time.

And so it goes lifetime over lifetime. A perfectly natural and stream-lined progression. Nothing to fear.

You may wonder why we share this now. The answer is simply it is time. With the Angel of Death hovering over your world, seemingly in overdrive, there is more focus on death, the unknown, and a great deal of leaning into fear which is counter productive.

Our intention is to ease your fears through this rudimentary explanation of your stages of beingness. It is not unknown as you've done it a great many times, you've simply forgotten.

Understand that no matter what stage you are in is Divinely aligned. You are loved and cared for, your team is with you, always guiding and comforting. **YOU ARE NEVER ALONE.**

There is truly nothing to fear. Even temporary discomfort as you adjust into or out of states of being is minimal. As much as possible, strive to remain in a state of flow rather than fear, that is the wise and most peaceful choice.

Know that a greater plan is at work. All is perfectly unfolding under the watchful eye of Creator and you will go on.

You are eternal, your experiences are temporary, and you have the power to shape them in ways that delight and please.

One day at a time, one choice at a time, you shape your tomorrows. It's totally up to you what you create. Keeping in mind that all actions have consequences (AKA karma), we highly recommend always making the best, most empowered choices so that your tomorrows are joyous and wonderful. If they're not, you know what to do…

And now your journey into the outer limits is coming to a close as you slowly drift back down into Earth's atmosphere, down past the clouds, and settle comfortably back into your body, retaining the memory and understanding you gained on this excursion through and beyond physical death.

Allow this expanded consciousness to bring you comfort in the difficult days ahead as you continue making the best, most powerful choices on your journey. It's not over till it's over and you've still got a lot of living to do.

So now it's time to come back to your third-dimensional life. Bring your consciousness back to your body as you wiggle your fingers and toes and allow yourself to be fully embodied once more. When you are ready open your eyes.

Just as promised you have returned from this strange journey safe and sound. Take your time processing what you have learned. You may wish to take all or parts of this meditative journey more than once so that you fully absorb all that has been encoded especially for you. Each time you will gain more insights. It is our hope and intention that you will feel more confident in yourself and your team as you lean into a state of peace and well being no matter what is happening around you.

You are deeply loved today, tomorrow, and for always.

Namasté Dear One

HOLIDAY PEACE MESSAGE

*B*eautiful, sparkling water, a lake. The water looks like Crystals as the light hits the top of it and glances off. So peaceful. You can hear the sound of waves hitting the shore gently, like a caress.

The sun shines on your face, warming you from outside in, from the top of your head to the tips of your toes. You're feeling Divine Love warming, energizing, refilling your energy stores so that *you* will be grounded, balanced, and filled with peace. Ready to step into the holiday season and a new exciting year to come.

Because, Dear One, know that the promise is it's going to be better next year. In fact, it's already better, because you have stepped forward on your spiritual journey. Your soul is awakening to the purpose for which you came. If you feel that excitement, know that the most important thing for you each and every day is to lean into love, peace, and harmony. Do your best to sidestep the conflicts. Don't involve yourself in them anymore than is absolutely necessary.

Stay on your path, looking up to the light, allowing yourself to be filled to overflowing with beautiful, Divine Love Light.

You are a gorgeous chalice, with your arms uplifted, golden white light flows down to you and fills you up. This time when it fills you up, it looks like tiny diamonds. Your whole being is filled up with tiny diamonds.

A metaphor for how precious you are. Think about what that means. *You* are a diamond, already perfect, polished. All you need do is accept and flow with the feeling of being loved far beyond what you can imagine.

You are in actuality, filled with healing, loving, light and energy.

All that you could ever want or ever need is available to you. Let go of stress, strain, and worry. Lean into love, letting your inner guide team support and nudge you in the right direction as needed.

Your angels need you to know they will always be there encouraging you forward on your path; delighting when you discover the juicy breadcrumbs they have scattered for you.

When you take action, they're cheering you on — your own personal cheering squad. Their only purpose for being is to help you on your awakening journey. Imagine all of that power and energy at your fingertips. What might you do with it?

When you relax and flow into that knowing, falling back into the warm, inviting arms of your team, they will carry you. They will get you through any challenge. Know on the other side of the challenge you're going to find firm ground again. You'll race forward with joy and delight at all the wonders experienced, and for all those around you. Because, as your energy overflows with the knowingness of who you are, love will flow abundantly from you to the world.

Those around you will be positively impacted. They too, will shift into a more positive outlook, or they will get out of the way, because it will be too uncomfortable for them.

So, those individuals in your life who regularly upset your apple cart? Know that by taking care of yourself, leaning into love and peace, then allowing it to flow from you, those individuals will begin to feel very uncomfortable in your presence and will soon leave.

They will no longer be an issue for you. This is the marvelous way you are cared for by your team and Creator.

How amazing is it that you're on this charmed journey? Everything works out for you. Yes, there will be challenges, but with your team's support you'll sail through any challenge.

You'll learn and grow and as you come through a challenge you'll be greeted by the wind and breeze caressing your face, gently lifting the locks of your hair, like fingers running through your hair. Such a beautiful, pleasant feeling, making you feel oh so cared for.

The trees nod and smile as you walk by, delighting in the energy emitting from you. For as you breath out, you feed the plants and trees. As they breath out, they feed you in this beautiful, harmonious Creation that takes care of your every need.

There you are, walking along this path looking to the horizon ahead. As you approach the horizon, you see your heart's desire, whatever that may be. You can almost touch it, you're so close.

Know that you will arrive there in Divine perfect timing. You are on your way. Your angels have promised to bring you together with your heart's desire, so move forward in faith and trust, allowing all of the delights of the world to satiate you, knowing as you move along that all of your needs are beautifully met.

Now, you're floating on a raft in the ocean. The water is calm. There are a few wispy clouds in the sky, for accents. There you lie, under a gorgeous sun with delightful day dreams floating through your mind.

Inspired by the Universe with new ideas and creations that you may choose to bring forth. It's important to allow yourself time to flow and float as you open yourself to receiving Divine inspiration.

When you're finished with your relaxing journey across the water, go back to your cozy space and write down those inspired ideas that were gifted to you.

They are building blocks that you will use to move closer to your heart's desire and beyond. Because there *will* be more. There's always more. That's why you're here. To embrace with exuberance all that life has to offer. Take those lusciously juicy berries and don't worry if they drip down your chin. Just enjoy the abundance the Universe dearly wants to share with you. Soak it up, enjoy, then move forward to experience even more.

Can you feel the glorious, springy grass under your bare feet? As you walk forward, hold out your arms and, maybe like Julie Andrews in *The Sound of Music* (Rodgers & Hammerstein musical, 1965) spin around and sing with unadulterated delight for all that you are and all that you're becoming; feeling so loved and cared for. That amazing sun is like the beaming face of your Creator looking down and delighting in who you are, because you're so beautiful, magnificent, and loved.

Creator delights in what you get up to. You were given this raw material and sent forth into the world to shape your life, in what-ever way you choose. New insights, ideas, joy, peace, harmony for yourself and for the entire world. There is not another like you in the multiverse. You are a gift.

Allow yourself to feel that truth deep inside so that it might spring forth in abundant love for yourself, and for the world. The light that shines from you will be a glorious beacon, drawing those who will enrich your life, bringing more joy and peace.

Flow through this delightful time of the year with excitement and anticipation as you step forward into the clean slate of a new year, beginning fresh with so much promise. It's a fresh opportunity to decide for yourself who you will be and what you will create in this new year.

Know that you can't get it wrong. This is about learning, experimenting, and expanding. That's why it's an awakening journey. You're learning and expanding all the time. As you walk forward on this beautiful journey, you're accompanied by a legion of angels, guides, enlightened beings, masters and teachers. All are available when you need assistance. No matter how small or large the issue, they are right there, Johnny on the spot, ready to assist. So allow yourself to float as you expand in wonder and delight, contemplating what you want to create in the new year. How will you use this opportunity?

Take your time. No need to decide right away. Allow inspiration to come. When it hits, treasure and hold it dear in your heart chakra. That seed will take root and blossom throughout the year into your inspired creation — your gift to self, and to the world.

Know that it is perfect, but you can change it anytime. Having made your choice, enjoy it — every last juicy drop.

When this creation feels complete, move on to the next glorious opportunity.

And thus it will ever be. That is why you're here, to be this expansive being. To bring your light into the world because *you* are a lightworker.

As you share love and light, it expands from you, to touch and impact others. Likewise, their light does the same for you.

Sharing and intermingling your beautiful love and light creates a wave of peace and harmony that expands across the planet, and it will keep getting better.

So, Dear One, as we conclude our journey, bring your energy and awareness back to your body. Know that all you have experienced is available to you whenever you need it. Just reach out and ask. Take the journey allowing it to evolve in whatever way your soul desires.

Subsequent journeys will be different as they and you continue expanding.

With massive love and blessings, your angels send kisses and hugs, enveloping you in love and in the safe, protected circle of their arms. You are oh so gloriously loved.

———⊸⋈⊷———

Take a couple of deep breaths, and when you're ready, open your eyes.

EPILOGUE

We are most pleased to present this meditation compilation to you, and gratified that you have partaken of our offer.

There is great hope for the future of humanity, with such as yourself awakening to the possibility of a bright future.

At this moment, there are many who shrink in fear, recoiling from the reality that surrounds them. It is too terrible to contemplate. (A vision of Ukrainians hiding from Russian soldiers. Afraid, but determined to fight to the death if necessary.)

There are also many who are oblivious. Their souls have not yet awakened. They don't believe that anything better awaits them. Their life is one long, bleak trail of futility.

For them we are sad, however, their day will come. If not this life-time, then another.

Meanwhile, there are more than enough lightworkers to facilitate the shift into Earthtopia. It's simply a matter of when they'll awaken to join in the cause.

It won't be long now. Events are accelerating, to the point where they will have to shift into awakening or miss the boat.

The acceleration you're noticing is a result of Earth, and you, shifting into fourth-dimensional beingness. It might feel as if you've stepped up to the mezzanine level and are operating from that space of awareness, while those not yet awakened remain on the ground floor.

Resist the temptation to look down upon them. They remain perfect souls, albeit behind you on the ascension path. Keep your eyes focused firmly on the path ahead, and they will do the same.

You will not be held back by them, but they may be inspired by you. See how that works? You cannot go back. This is a one-way journey ever forward.

The past exists as reference points so that you might learn from it. It is not intended that you get sucked back in, because that would leave you mired in the muck, bitterly regretting your choice to engage with what was.

Besides, so many magnificent adventures await on the path ahead. Turning back would deprive you of all that awaits.

Should you feel the need for shoring up, remember these meditative experiences. Select one that matches your present needs and use it. This collection is a powerful tool, addressing a wide-range of situations and needs.

In the future, when you revisit a meditation, because it will be familiar, you may wish to turn off the recording and allow yourself to freely move forward. Should the images or scene change, flow with it. When you do this, you open the door for your angels to bring more insights and more clarity.

Look upon these meditative journeys as open-ended adventures. The structure is there to get you started. However, *it's your journey.*

The guided visuals are but a launching point to prime the pump and help you smoothly slip into the experience.

Once you're in, connected and comfortable, allow yourself to explore anything new that shows up.

We highly suggest you record your experience of these journeys in as much detail as possible so that later you can analyze, looking for a deeper message than you might have noticed in the moment.

Messages are always multilayered.

Some of your meditative journeys will be learning opportunities, as your angels teach you principles you may not yet have encountered. Even more important to record them, as what you do not understand in the moment will one day come into focus.

As you gather the individual pieces and put them together, you'll find that they form a larger picture. The full message may only be revealed once you put those pieces together.

We use this building block approach to teaching so that you can logically ascend, one step at a time, and not get overwhelmed.

Should overwhelm rear its ugly head, select a meditation that's easy and fun, like a canoe ride down a slow-moving river.

Sometimes what you most need is a respite to catch your breath, regroup, analyze, or just be. You need to maintain balance lest you upset your own applecart.

Whatever it is you need, we are here to serve. It is our honor and privilege to do so. That is our role in the grand scheme of the Universe.

When you need a break from the intensity of life, try a little grounding exercise. Do some relaxing and deep breathing. Then call out to your angels asking for a fun adventure. They'll happily oblige. Remember, your experiences in the fifth dimension are as real as your third or fourth-dimensional life.

Want to travel? Ask your angels to take you wherever you want to go. Yes, you can do that! If present life circumstances do not allow you to travel, then go through the fifth dimension.

You see? We want to expand your awareness of what is possible. In the fifth dimension, everything happens at the speed of thought. No limitations. Go have your adventures and enjoy them to the hilt.

Practicing and becoming adept now will pay dividends in the future as you go through even more trying times on the road to Earthtopia.

You've already come far on your ascension journey. Once in a while, reflect upon who you were when you started. Then marvel and appreciate the incredible progress.

Now, contrast that with the progress to come... yes, incomprehensible from your present vantage point, and that's as it should be.

You do need to be mindful of living in the present. However, once in a while, it's a good idea to look ahead in anticipation of the phenomenal life journey **YOU** are creating.

Your adventures in the fifth dimension are like dress rehearsals, helping you to prepare so that you'll be ready for whatever challenges come your way.

About that travel... if your desire is to travel to a place that in the third dimension is inhospitable, *allow your angels to take you to a future version of that place*, where it's everything you hoped it would be.

Just bear in mind that when that future day arrives, it may look different, as those timelines are still being written. What you see will be the idealized version from an angelic perspective.

Who knows, that may inspire you to have a hand in bringing your vision to fruition. After all, *you* are the creator of your reality. Until now, that reality has been limited by your understanding of what is possible.

Are you getting the picture that *everything* is possible?

Ok now, we've given you a lot to think about. Let's tie it up in a bright red bow (referencing root chakra and being grounded), that you can take away.

There are more possibilities available in the multiverse than you have yet to imagine. When you reach full fourth-dimensional being-ness, the contrast to third-dimensional reality will be night and day.

From that perspective, you may grasp just how much more is yet possible.

But that's getting a bit too far ahead. Suffice to say, there are some mind-blowing experiences ahead as you step into the greater potential your soul planned for this lifetime.

Auf wiedersehen for now, Metatron and the Gang

Metatron likes to mix up the sign-offs for fun. In case you aren't familiar with the phrase, Auf wiedersehen is German for *until we meet again.*

AFTERWORD

When I asked Metatron if there was anything else he wanted to share before we wrapped this book up, he delivered the boundary-busting message below, especially for you.

We see the challenges you bravely face. If it were possible to take this burden from you, we most assuredly would. However, then you would be deprived of the learning and spiritual growth.

So you see, even though we, and you, might prefer to skip this part of human history, it is necessary. It *does* serve a greater purpose, and the benefits will be felt across the multiverse.

If you ever doubted your connection to all that is, this is your evidence.

You are like a speck of sand in the vastness of the multiverse, yet you hold the power to greatly impact, to create ripples which will be felt in galaxies far away.

As you step up to higher consciousness, higher vibrational frequency, and a deeper understanding of yourself and the cosmos, keep in mind that these are not trivial matters.

You are doing profoundly deep, sacred work.

I've long said this is a consequential lifetime. Perhaps now you're getting an inkling of what that means for you personally, and for the world at large?

This is why it is vitally important that you stand in your power, love, faith, and trust. Keep moving forward every day. With each step, you move closer to the glorious day when Earthtopia will be fully realized.

In the meanwhile, you'll see wisps and hints as it manifests around you.

Sometimes you might feel as if you're walking around with your head in the clouds — vision obscured. Yet, every now and then, you'll bounce upward to catch a glimpse of what's above the clouds. In that split second, you'll see the ongoing formation of Earthtopia.

With your intention and efforts, you are co-creating that new reality. Like a dream that will come to life in Divine, perfect timing.

All the pieces are already there. Laid out for you so that you'll be able to avail yourself as needed. It is all within your grasp. A potential future being crafted by your thoughts and actions. Now that's some powerful juju. (Said with a wink.)

All this and more, already a part of your reality, slowly coming into focus.

As you experience the meditations we have prepared for you, your consciousness and reality will expand. Allow yourself to flow with the words.

When listening to the audio, if your vision moves in another direction, stop the recording, and follow the energy. For once you plug into angel guidance, you open the door to deeper downloads, and greater inspired opportunities.

Your vision of self is being broken wide open. You are no longer the small, limited version of yourself you used to know. No, you have expanded far beyond that reality.

We've been teasing at the edges of your psyche, lighting little fires of inspiration to encourage you to take the lid off your box and discover the greater truth of who you are.

All of that potential bottled up, waiting for the right moment to come bursting forth like a carbonated beverage that's been shaken. (Wink)

You can no longer settle for playing small, for limiting yourself to the boundaries of what you thought of as your world.

That will no longer be enough. A deep hunger for more grows within you even now. And everything you desire to sate that hunger already exists.

A veritable buffet of selections, each more delicious than the last. No, my magnificent child, your days of settling are past.

What of those who have not yet had this awakening, you may wonder. We say, do not worry and fret over them. They'll awaken just as you, in Divine timing.

When you find yourself straying into worry and doubt, reflect upon the lessons you've learned, the magnificent manifestations you've witnessed, the heart-bursting joy you've felt. Revel in it, knowing that even more and better awaits. Keep your eyes focused steadily on the path ahead.

Just a little distance ahead, though, you don't want to get ahead of yourself and miss the delightfully exquisite experiences of the present.

Your angels are even now squealing with delight as they celebrate your progress, because *they* know what's around the next bend. You'll soon enough get there. Based upon their celebrations, you are going to be over the moon delirious.

Yep, that's just a hint of your grand future. (Big smile)

Talk soon, Metatron

WHAT COMES NEXT?

A FAVOR

If you found value in this book, would you consider writing a review on Amazon or GoodReads? It needn't be long, just your honest opinion. Or, if you prefer, even a star rating would make a tremendous difference.

By adding your review/rating, you'll make it possible for more lightworkers to discover Metatron's message and accelerate the journey to Earthtopia.

Your words could be the ones to help another lightworker find their own purposeful path. With your help, we'll create some massive ripples in the pond.

JANUARY 2023, 21-DAY MEDITATION CHALLENGE

In January 2023, Debbra plans to host a group *21-Day Meditation Challenge* in the Facebook support group. If you're ready to fast-track your own channeling voice, please join us. Whether it's your first time, or a repeat, the growth potential is tremendous.

Be sure to read *The Path to Hearing Angels & Guides* before joining so that you'll be ready to start on Day 1.

MORE CHANNELED GUIDANCE

You'll find monthly forecasts for lightworkers on Debbra's YouTube channel and on Medium.com.

FUTURE CHANNELED BOOKS

Watch for more channeled books forthcoming from Archangel Metatron to continue supporting and teaching the lightworkers of the world.

ABOUT THE AUTHOR

Debbra Lupien, is an Author, Spiritual Teacher, and Voice of the Akashic Records.

She previously authored the international best-selling, *Akasha Unleashed: The Missing Manual To You*, which has become a global catalyst for personal transformation. Her more recent books include: *The Path to Hearing Angels & Guides: 21-Days of Meditation*, and the companion workbook: *Metatron's 21-Day Meditation Challenge*.

Debbra believes the holy grail of your soul journey is: Find what feeds your soul — and DO IT. Wise souls take the shortcut found in the Akashic Records.

Besides authoring books, Debbra regularly shares channeled messages, meditations, and spiritual lessons on her YouTube channel and Medium.com.

When not journeying in the fifth dimension, she enjoys traveling, hiking, and spending time with her horses and family at their mountaintop home.

Debbra is available for private readings, speaking engagements, and live channeled events.

Reach out to her through her website: AkashaUnleashed.com or via email: Answers@AkashaUnleashed.com

POPULAR LIVE EVENTS

Join her the 1st Monday of each month for *Metaphysical Chat Livestream* on YouTube at 7pm EST, where you can bring your questions about all things metaphysical and she'll channel the answers.

Or, sign up to her VIP list (https://AkashaUnleashed.com/VIP), for a personal Zoom invite to an *Ask Your Guides Live* event, each 3rd Saturday at 11am EST, for *complimentary mini readings*.

facebook.com/AkashaUnleashed
twitter.com/AkashaUnleashed
instagram.com/debbralupien
youtube.com/debbralupien

ACKNOWLEDGMENTS

TO METATRON'S WARRIORS

The dedicated lightworkers of the 21-Day Meditation Challenge, who support and encourage as we all march towards Earthtopia together.

I had no idea when we began the challenge how the group would coalesce and expand into a global support network for one another and for Gaia.

My heart is full of gratitude for your love and commitment. Thank you.

TO MELINDA VAN FLEET

Who graciously invited me to channel on her Good Karma Success Coach Podcast. Chapters 8, 13, and 18 are only some of those beautiful meditations. Thank you for your wisdom, confidence, and support, you're my hero.

ALSO BY DEBBRA LUPIEN

Akasha Unleashed: The Missing Manual to You

The Path to Hearing Angels & Guides: 21 Days of Meditation

Metatron's 21-Day Meditation Challenge Workbook

Co-Authored Books:

The Wellness Universe Guide to Complete Self-Care: 25 Tools for Stress Relief

Unscripted: How Women Thrive in Life, Business, and Relationships

Conscious Creators Magazine: Discover the Secrets of Awakened Women

NOTES

NOTES

NOTES

NOTES

NOTES

Manufactured by Amazon.ca
Bolton, ON